More Outbursts

From the Seventh Decade

A collection of poems by
Carol Chapman

MORE OUTBURSTS: FROM THE SEVENTH DECADE

A COLLECTION OF POEMS BY CAROL CHAPMAN

Copyright © 2025 by Carol Chapman

ISBN-13: 979-8-9931588-0-8
Paperback Edition: October 2025

ISBN-13: 979-8-9931588-1-5
Kindle edition: October 2025

LCCN: 2025921664

Printed in the United States of America

Editor: Laurie Chandlar
Publisher: Chandlar Creative, New York, NY 10075

Cover design: Kim Killion, Killion Group Inc.

*This collection is dedicated to all my readers
who find the poems engaging and
thought-provoking, and to newcomers
who are discovering the joys
and challenges of poetry.
Proving, once again, that poetry
has a place in our lives.*

Table of Contents

Foreword

I met Carol just a couple of years ago at the salon in our Yorkville neighborhood as we both were getting manicures. Leave it to New York City to bring together two souls in a random way, sharing some of the keenest, artful values. We started meeting regularly to talk about writing, books, and creativity. Carol regaled me with stories of her travels and her varied experiences in life. She is fearless and dances her way around the world. Her life has been a reflection of her poetry and vice versa. Without words exchanged, I could have told you she was a poet.

Words are, in fact, Carol's lifeblood. I remember the day, sitting in her living room drinking Prosecco, when she wondered out loud if she could publish a book of poems. I vehemently said, "I think you should do it! No time like the present!" So she did. Like the maverick she is, after several months of collecting her work and finding a publisher, she released *Outbursts: From the Seventh Decade*, started up an Instagram account, and held signings and speaking engagements. This time around, I wanted to work with her as a team. I am delighted to share this sequel with you.

Carol is real, honest, and diligent in her wordsmithing. She is relevant to today and brings her decades to bear on our age of uncertainty. Carol is brooding, dark, full of dire warning…yet she is also full of sunshine, sultry fire, and hope. A firecracker of a lady, it's no mistake that there are fireworks on the cover. This book is a reflection of life right now, as a whole, brimming over in grit and soul. It reminds us that life is stunning and we best not waste it. So find your favorite place, curl up, and enjoy the adventure of *More Outbursts*.

—Laurie Chandlar

Forsythia

Early darkness recedes
Lengthening day encourages
    Sprinting feet
    Widening eyes

    Tulips pop up
Displaying vibrant turbans
    Standing erect
    Signaling Spring
    Tidy and regal

    Forsythia
Splashes yellow
An outlier in Nature's repertoire
Trumpeting Spring with blooming flowers
    Leaves an afterthought

    A chorus with a clustering instinct
Regaling the eye
Sprawling like a Jackson Pollock yellow

Its breathtaking singularity defies conformity
    Nature's gift
    Outlier in our midst

Bereft

Looking like a still life
        Empty bird's nest
            Dislodged

Stooped to pick it up
        Cradle it
Admire its intricate craftsmanship

Thinking about a frantic bird's loss
        No place to lay eggs
        No place to nurture hatchlings
Nature's rhythm disrupted

Walking on city sidewalks
        Eyes sting
Men and women nesting on concrete
        No comforting bed
        No soothing blankets
Nature's most sophisticated species

        Bereft
                Security   Human   Dignity

        DENIED

NULL AND VOID

Trumpet the sanctity of women's bodies
Use brains and brawn to thwart
Taliban mentality
Picture Iranian women tossing
the hijab into the wind

Ramp up the demand for an
equal rights amendment
Expose hypocritical pronouncements
and double standards
Blast governmental overreach — gatekeeping
women's bodies

PROCLAIM

Women will not be stamped NULL AND VOID

NO   Supreme Decrees

NO   Abortion Legislation

NO   Venerating the Uterus

Feel the PURPLE in your veins
Resist with every fiber of your being

SHOUT OUT...
HELL NO!!!

Snatched

Words cut like steel –

Pointedly selected to deliver

Expunging words chosen

    Violates

        sanctity of mind
        diminishing subtlety or potency

          distorting intent

Words

    Snatched
    Consigned to darkness

Replacements — hollow scarecrows

Micromanagers dueling with creative process

      Ruptures the spleen

Hope

Hope the thing with spiky spines
Camps on my window sill

A barrier to sinister encroachments
Spines cluster
Protecting fleshy cactus stem

Herbivores thwarted
Source of water guarded
Stem thrives

Spiky phalanx ensures stem survival
Defeating arid environment

Under siege people must be
Protective spiky spines

Clustering to repel harsh suffocating decrees
Shielding society's vulnerable stem
From rapacious omnivores draining
Stem's vitality
Siphoning its lifeblood
Leaving a limp citizenry

Hope is the cactus residing in our spine.

Magical Isle

Arriving on Governors Island quickens my heart
     Every season is unique

A seagull on my bike path
     Basking in summer's warmth
     Sounds of squealing children
Under technicolor skies

Lavender — purple's alter ego
     Perfuming the air

Wild flowers — abundant greenery

Purple Coneflowers in Leggett Terrace
All resplendent and on display

Fall brings decompression
A costume change begins
Green bows to golden and reddish hues

Sun begins its shift
     Winter solstice brings drama
     Grey skies cast alluring shadows
Cycling in winter light sharpens perception

Visitors become infrequent
A stillness settles— allowing one's mind
      To embark on a contemplative journey
      In a magical landscape
With a dusky sky overhead

Cautionary Tales

Ear-splitting voices sucking oxygen
from the air
Sound bites honed on whetstones
become Orwell's newspeak —
a vocabulary of counterfeit words
conjuring a new Babylon,
gnawing on comity,
shifting the earth's tectonic plates

Babel ON....

Focusing on your rippling wavelets...
I hear murmuring
A monologue from the edge of the horizon

Breath like rotting compost
from the ocean's depths
fills my lungs with its richness,
reminding me that I am steeped
in earth and water

Your waves develop jagged peaks
trashing the shore

woefully enraged —
roaring in my ears

trumpeting your grievances —

no ark will withstand your onslaught

Jamaican Tapestry

Savoring Blue Mountain coffee
while perusing my journal brings back
scenes and images
woven in words like a tapestry

Climbing to Saint Ann's Parish
rust-red bauxite
and textured rocks are nature's painting
gracing the highway
A local road leads to Fern Gulley
lifted by sea breezes
ferns sway in a chorus line

NOW
I see myself walking along a
rock-strewn path
trimmed with greenery
leading to Holywell Falls
a scuttering cascade
hidden below the path
behind the streaming water
a rainbow on a granite

canvas teased me with its fleeting presence

My journal takes me to the sea of paradise
shades of turquoise delighted me
evoking the spirituality of Robert Ryman's
shades of white

Inhaling the sea's essence
feeling it in my pores
remembering my dance before it
wind whipping my hair — transports me

Bathed by the images in my Jamaican tapestry
I am humbled by nature's artistry and blessed
by the mystical isle

Technicolor Bruise

Pulsating purple   electric blue

Love's center shifts

Becoming yellow

Seeping into one's mental landscape

Leaving a technicolor bruise

A presence declaring its visibility

Mocking an artless lover's vow

Absence does not expunge a lover's being

Silence does

Shed a Tear

Listening to Arvo Parte's Alina
A backdrop for mining thoughts

    Family   Friends

Evaporated
Distilled

Leaving
        Words spoken
        Deeds accomplished
        Love to cherish

Shed a tear
        Weapons mushroom
        Bombs indiscriminate
        Lives severed

    Shed tears

            A deadly species

Tramples

Defiles

    Decency
Blistering words
Conjuring an elixir of hate

       Shed tears as our planet roils…

Whispering

Whisper

     to tamp down rage
     to neutralize bullies
     to soften the edge
     of conflicting points of view

Whisper

     to deflect wounding words
     to stanch evil intentions
     to steady oneself in challenging
     situations

Whisper

     into the ear of a loved one
     into a gentle breeze until cradled
     in a hush

Beware —the Jabberwock

Simulated   Unctuous   Voices
        Alexa   Siri — Jubjub birds

                Mimicking humanness
                Corroding autonomy
                Stymieing initiative

Chatbot — a sterile computer program

Artificial conversationalist — supplanting human
discourse
Robotically responding to questions
                Simulating a human voice

Ongoing incursions

        Slithering Chatbot GPT
Pretrained transformer capable of challenging
        So-called misconceptions
Reconfiguring human thinking — invading minds

Galumping   Burbling   AGI

        Artificial General Intelligence

Primed to outperform human intellect

Insuring mankind's obsolescence

    Thinking   Reasoning
                 SNARED
Threatening human viability

    BEWARE the JAWS and CLAWS
OF THE JABBERWOCK

Invisible

Freedom of expression demonized
Kent State shadow stalks campuses

Inferno chars human lives
       physically
       emotionally
       mentally

Eyes see
Voices cry out

Weeping Willows
       Winnowed like chaff

Visible — masks invisible

Resilience

Navigating through life
Like balancing on one foot
Requires

Strength
Resistance
Defiance

WHIRLWINDS

Prejudice
Malice
Grievance
Fear

Topple civility
Fracture unity
Mock sobriety

Avoid Dante's frozen lake
Souls encased in ice

Counterbalance the WHIRLWINDS
    Forbearance
    Forgiveness
    Love

Lives entwined
    Dancing together
        Maintaining the center

Kingston, Jamaica

Downtown fleet street a mural mecca
Projecting images of inner-city life
Like flash cards
      On otherwise derelict walls
      Artists and volunteers of all stripes
Incarnating the spirit of Bob Marley
An open-air space transformed
Becomes a hub of self and pride
A happening where Shango
          Inspired with a vision of an ongoing
      Art project
          Extends his thumb and forefinger
      To a captivated stranger soaking up

Reality
Strength
Possibility
Ingredients of a Kingston stew

OBLIVION

There is NO
>ONE THERE

No twinkle in the eyes
No wry smile
No connective tissue
>Nothing to share

No spirit
>Only empty shoes

RED LIGHT...GREEN LIGHT

Red light ... Green light
A game children play
        freeze or advance
to reach a goal by listening.

Gaming
an adult version
        tramples affections

Toying
        leaches toxin with consequences

Ghosting
another variation of the game
        ushers in finality.

A tone-deaf player mired in self-indulgence avoids
Listening
        a vital component in the game.

Red becomes a permanent signal
Green fades

An absent player
     skewers relationships
     shrivels connections

No maneuvers left
     just a loser.

Life In Stasis

Light streams into a room
      Cleansing
      Dressing
      Adorning

Earrings never neglected
No external sounds resonating
Only the prism of light
      Bathing the senses

Friends detached
      Sterile voices
Timbreless words encased in a device

Inducement to dash into the street cauldron nullified
Invigorating gallery hop in Chelsea a chimera

Tormenting thoughts of a lover floating in a
fishbowl of exile
      Cannot be expunged
Just drifting in a timeless vacuum confronted by
      Circumstances deadbolt

Waiting and longing for release from life in stasis

Rain Telegraphs

Rain telegraphs to a semi-conscious brain
        tapping like ballerinas on toes

                Wind cranks up
Symphonic sound crackling
                        tunnels down window panes

Rain douches streets
            dislodging curb detritus
            wiping sooty grime from windshields

Parched gardens swamped in a title wave
            No need to rouse
                        Or
            peek through blinds

Skyscape in foreboding grey—blackness
            permeates eyelids
Rain's staccato
            fades as Hypnos descends.

Walking with John Noble

If you stroll through ancient cemeteries eying
aged granite stone
tilted and fallen markers of once vital lives

     John Noble would give an approving nod

A young man sailed on the Anna Sophia into
the boneyard of wrecked
forgotten ships and never turned away

He spent a lifetime chronicling dying sailing
ships in limestone
     Masts and hulls splintered
     rigging dangling
     clinging to remnants of a perishing vessel

Black and white lithographs capture detail
     casting shadows on rotting wood
a behemoth's slow descent into murky waters

John Noble's crayon touched the stone
with grim reality
artistic precision breathing life into a bygone era

Noble's maritime lithographs
are the stone mausoleums
marking the history of sailing vessels
and the rugged men
who sailed in the "Hulls and Hulks" of time

Hawkness

Sighted a hawk
Perched in a tilted tree
Wondered if he felt the slant
Hawk eyes focused
On — I know not
Maybe prey or just surveying
territory
His stillness is hypnotic
A powerful hawk
Calm
Detached
Afterall — he is a hawk

Ecstasy

Being stroked by a divining rod

dousing sacred lips
       Male seeking treasure

Lips quiver mouths suck

      Earth quakes
          feverish shaking
electrified limbs

      Bodies intertwined

Insatiable tongues   libidinous lips

    in a millisecond

a tsunami

inseparable souls
       rafting on a wave's crest

Immunity

Has anyone noticed?

Politicians
Wrap themselves in presumed immunity
Nothing matters in the airtight bubble

G u n   m a n i a
Says who?   Delusionists!

Nothing to do with assault weapon availability
A covenant allowing purchase of the AR-1

Children
Victims of gun violence
No protection

　　　Gun obsession haunts the nation

No immunity from stalkers seeking to draw blood
Leaving limp children in their wake

A nation anesthetized

Shock value diluted by repetition

Andy Warhol's Orange Car Crash Fourteen Times

Surpassed by incalculable numbers of children
Slaughtered in their sanctuary

No rationality
No empathy

NO Response

Zyning

Zyn nicotine pouches
in an innocuous white tin
targeting children
in a secret world of online gaming

spinning a nickname guaranteed
to grab attention

    LIP CUSHIONS

Conjuring merriment more deadly
than the slick ad

    Call for Philip Morris

Hucksters — now influencers
Seeping into young lives using algorithms

    — precision bombs

Peddling addiction
Gaming defenseless children

zyninfluencing with zyn videos

A new game board embedded in the old game
using the most powerful hook ever imagined

Embraced

Jamaica's embrace
      reaches out like a conjuror
Flame of the forest
      peeks out from velvety green carpeting
Olympians
      Watchful
      Sheltering
      Shimmering in sunrise and sunset
         cloak the Rock

Nature's canvas teases the eye
      Bequeaths calmness
In the mirror of mortality

Song of Deliverance

A directionless soul haunting the moors

Filled with regrets
      anger
      self-loathing
Follows a terrain pocked by sinkholes

Desperation twists and mangles —
A struggling drifter succumbs
Clawing and writhing is useless
Boogeymen cling
      distorting reality
      clouding acumen
      smothering humanity

Wailing and deflecting blame for
self-inflicted wounds
Weighs down any attempt to climb out
of desolation's maw

A song of deliverance has no hostile lyrics

Leave the smoldering hatred

and the moor behind
Reach out to a hand that has
     No skin tone
     No gender identity
     No religious signature

Grasp the hand that clasps your wrist
Allow light to sear the boogeymen
Emerge purged from the sinkhole
     Singing the Song of Deliverance

Ringmaster

A barker outside the forum

    shouts

    cajoles

fills the cavernous arena

This modern-day Colosseum packs 20,000 souls
    shoulder to shoulder
Rivals the pageantry of the gladiatorial heyday
    fanfare
        confetti
    balloons
        rallying cries
    music elevating heart beats

stirring the blood for the contest ahead

Gladiators joust while the Ringmaster tap dances
    words CRACK exclaiming no mercy

Public acclaim demands entertainment

spiked with blood
seasoned with venom

Submissive gladiators
thirsting for the blood-stained
          palm of glory
          soft shoe
into the ringmaster's clutches
          unwittingly step on a boomerang

babbling voices dwindle
puddling at the conjuror's feet

Drowning

The soil under my feet is sinking even though the
sun still rises in the East
I wake up when it
        peeks through the blinds

Unsettled by a dawn that holds no promise
only a deadened beat of a drum marshaling
leaden feet
        seared by blistering words

Words oozing from mouths mocking truth
leaching the soils nutrients

        Creating mayhem
invigorating long simmering hatreds
always poised to erupt

        Drowning rule of law
Excoriating reason with incendiary rhetoric

        A murky version of truth
        scorches my eyes

        drawing my feet into a swamp

Love In the Purple Zone

Ours was an unbidden magnetic attraction

atoms in a chemical reaction
        releasing energy

We embraced the moment without reservation
                One radiating electric red
        the other cool lapis

Desire softly encircled my torso
        breaching a barrier
        drawing me into a purple zone

Ultimately — tormenting   fragmenting
        a loving heart
                Purple never dims

Musings
(for the 21C and BEYOND)

during after and beyond corona

APPLEFIED

iPhones   tablets

Video Gaming

LIFE DEATH H O M O G E N I Z E D

theater   movies

NETFLIXED

concerts   bookstores

SPOTIFIED   AMAZONED

GOOGLE'S

DOSSIER

EMBALMED
            by
                    ZOOM

FULSOME
                    DIGITAL VOICES

            AI   TAKEOVER

MINDS   EMOTIONS   BODIES

SHRINK   WRAPPED

Undine Olive

Jubalana morphed into Bibs XYZ
       Shielding identity
Until Undine Olive emerged from murky depths

She balked when a phalanx of personas
       Envy in their eyes
Threatened a coup

Clinging to her birthright —
       Undine staked her turf
Goggles were stalking — bludgeoning mavericks

Undine clung like a barnacle to her identity
       In lockstep Goggles surrounded her

She pleaded for her existence
       Voicing opposition to endless encryption

Defying GOOGLIZATION — REBELLIOUS
       UNYIELDING

Undine — DECRYPTED

Rendering the battalion powerless

Expectations

It takes a decade to become a master teacher
To be jumping out of one's shoes with
Anticipation
Anxiety
Excitement
Feeling the adrenaline rush
When September rolls around
Blackboard looms
   Chalk in hand
I write
   I respect you — you respect me
     you respect each other
   Escape your mental zip code

Discussion gets off to a rollicking start
Teacher imparts a vision of a just
way to negotiate life — beginning in our classroom

Now — everything seems lopsided
I wake up each morning hearing about

Injustice
Hatred
Political division

I see myself in the mirror as an emoji
Downturned lips
A teardrop streaming from my eye

I buck-up to face expectations of exuberant students
        In our classroom

Eclipse

Darkness in daylight
Moon glides between
Earth and Sun
Millions of eyes focused
On Nature's phenomenon

Sun bowing out
Reappearing in minutes

Darkness remains
Myopic eyes
Shun the shroud strangling light

Ignore leeching blight
Targeting — diversity inclusion equality

Falsehoods enshrined
Climate change winked
Truth withered

Reason and empathy shunned
Darkness flows lava-like
Total eclipse

Something Strange Happened

Setting out for my walk
enveloped in a murky haze
smitten
by malignant forces
focused on dissolution

Approaching the vicinity of
the venerable museum
something strange begins to happen
my body feels relief
coaxing me to walk towards
the beckoning steps

Wrapped in silence
brisk air lifts my spirit
My body floats along
like a cloud

Barriers seem illusory
nothing hinders me

My massless body enters seamlessly
into a corridor
Greek and Roman figures

greet my shadowless self
I navigate through
the hushed cathedral of art
to commune with sculptural rocks
in the garden court
basking in their presence
my loss of corporeality seems natural

I visit the Temple of Dendur
Slip through the glass into the park
where trees are my limbs and torso

My new self moves to a performance hall
dulcet sounds reverberate

Taking a ghostly position
my roots swell in disbelief
Instruments performing
a bow caressing strings
a cello mimicking a human voice
an oboe's sleek body emitting eerie sounds

I head for the plaza
a tenor's voice reverberates
off surrounding buildings

An overflowing audience
of arboreal ghosts playfully
inhabiting each other's space
welcomes me

Stung

Eyes seduced by seductive greenery
and a cloud-stippled sky,
        feet floating on crisp morning air
                I step off the ferry —
Seemingly from nowhere
        A wasp stings with fury
Piercing an idyllic setting
        deflating ego
        causing pain

Why target Me in this motley group?
A senseless — but familiar refrain deriding
a random occurrence

Uncertainty's calling card
        a jarring reminder
        delivered in a split second
        by a wasp's sting

Gaia's Uprising

Wild turkeys send a clarion call from Gaia
Squirrels leap from trees
Coyotes yelp
Deer peek-out from underbrush

    Call Intensifies

Bees swarm
Hawks descend

All lured by turkeys' sense of urgency

    Earth's mother

Enraged by two-legged usurpers
fueled by greed
arrogantly flipping
earth's climate switch

    Proclaims an uprising

Rebellious fauna
Smoldering heat
Torrential rain

Cyclonic winds

Designed to bring two-legged defilers
to the brink of extinction

Restoring nature's rhythm in
Gaia's dominion

Revolt

A planet's rage slaps
Pokes out eyes
No safety valve
Water flows over the edge

Oceans   seas   rivers   lakes

In revolt

Lips salt-encrusted lock
Eyes plead...roaring decibels crush eardrums
Feet collapse
Ripped from the earth's womb

Oceans — a gorge in the throat
of human centrism

Blitz

Incendiary bombs spewed

> **Demonize**
> **Humiliate**
> **Deceive**

Festering mouths

> **Salivate**

Specious words stoke

> **Fear**
> **Hatred**
> **Violence**

Ulcerated tongues

Subjugate the populace
Wreak havoc with a nation's integrity

Smother the rule of law

> **Leaving piles of rubble**

BLITZKRIEG

Joker

Court jester devolves – no longer truth-teller
            cloaked in humor
No laser wit mocking king's overreach

Critic or guardian

        Court fool targeting incompetence

                sputters   vanishes

Drought and Dust
                Fashion a new breed

        Leavened with egotism and cankerous hate

Three-pointed hat swapped
                for orange wig

Microphone amplifies buffoonery
                        cheesy theatricality
Joker trolls for April fools

        Smoldering embers of racism flare up
fanned by scurrilous name calling

acolytes   spew
contagious breath

Catapulting a hollow scarecrow
onto a plinth ruptured by cognitive distortion

A joker for the 21st century gnaws on decency
gleefully scrambles social norms

steps back grinning
as the stage
implodes

Nightmare

Man-made nightmare
  Seasoned with devil's venom
  Flows like spilt coffee
    Smothering light
    Blanketing reason
    Injecting cruelty

Puffed-up egos
Spreading blistering lies
Stoke fear

Man-made nightmare encircles the powerless
    Victimizing
    Dehumanizing

Smirking — spewing incendiary words
  While feasting on spoils
  Concocting more terrifying torture

Uncertainty hovers like polluted air
  Consequences inescapable

    Nightmarish
      Like Allegator Alcatraz
      And Dachau

Lullaby

Truth — grey washed
      steeped in fog of lunacy

Sycophants metastasize
      Zuckering facts
            kneeling before emperor

Earth's death throes pooh-poohed

      Lullabye — Drill Baby Drill
            lulling earthlings

Live clips depicting
      treacherous assault
Touted as exuberance

      Not Caesarism

Books excoriated

    B A N N E D

Ideas — lead to contemplation
      introspection
      discernment

Saturating minds with Wokeism

AVOID enlightenment

Induce coma with lullabies scripted

For hooligans wearing
proud insignia

Banned

Fahrenheit 451's flames
　　Leap off the page

Handmaiden's Tale
　　　　1984

　　Beloved　　The Blood Years

　　　　All Boys Aren's Blue

　　Romeo and Juliet

TOURCHED IN THE FLAMES

Savonarola
　　　　　self-righteous arbiter
　　　　　of correctness in our midst

Enlightenment highjacked

　　　　Inquiring minds cloaked

　　　　Free thought shackled

No dark chapters

　　　Only smoldering ashes.

Porch Alchemy

Words bounce off porch boards
    Ideas shared
    Connections and contradictions discovered

A heady brew infiltrates our space
    Dissolving barriers —

Giddiness skips along the boards
as Ulyssess, Carol, and David
    Feel the transformative power
    Words freely expressed
    Freedom to connect

Soulmates — no base metal — just pure gold.

On The Lanai

Pygmy rattlesnake sitting on the lanai
    Playfully twirling straws
        awaiting small prey

Dusky camouflage masks intent
    an ambush calculated to overwhelm
Snake slithers
    pounces
    devours

A musky scent trails behind the pygmy
    marking territory
    leaving sweetish stench
    overpowering the pygmy

Cowering pygmy snake flounders
    shedding dusky skin
    writhing to sluff off

        invasive musky odor
        polluting the lanai

Visitation

Sitting on a bench
    Basking in stillness

Newspaper draped on my lap
    Thoughts like a jigsaw puzzle

Flash of orange and black
    Lands on my paper

Antennae and eyes lock
    Departure as swift as arrival

No monarch ever sighted
    In my sanctuary

Your reassuring guise
    Telegraphed my way forward

BLOODTHIRST

ATTACK

> Slaughter
> Rape
> Kidnapping
> Blazing hatred

Nations's sanctity violated — atrocities

> Screams reverberate

REVENGE

Drinking from the bloodthirsty
Enemy's cup

Mother, Father, Sister, Brother...
Limp bodies
No comforting arms

Children cowering in innocence
Stench of death suffocating hope

Unguided bombs cannot resurrect
Victims of terror

Human shield mantra
No justification

RETRIBUTION

A hamster wheel endlessly spinning
Splashing blood as the cup overflows
While the world inhales …

Rose Eugene

When she walked into Lew's room
at the nursing home
Rose carried herself with confidence

Residents were comforted
Her smile was sunlight dancing in the room

Our reunion happened on a scorching afternoon
       we sat face to face
          slipped into easy catch-up conversation

Life had not always been kind to Rose

An auto accident
in which a man lost his legs still haunts her

She has never been able to place herself in a
driver's seat
But this horror gave her
       Empathy and compassion for human life

Rose is Haitian
arrived in our midst at age twelve

She has   spirit   talent   fortitude — like pioneers
        who preceded her

Rose is a wholehearted American, but more
important —
she is a precious human being.

Her life is a reminder that America's gate

should not be a deadlock

I was fortunate to have a nurse practitioner caring
for Lew
who brought honor to her profession

Apparitions

Apparitions moving through
my sitting room appeared

before my eyes
like my gull carrying a fish for breakfast
looking for a place to feast

My gull demanded stillness

I became rooted

in the landscape — spellbound

observing regal beauty tearing flesh

My apparitions demanded meditative silence
enabling me to feast on memory

Shadows comforting and disturbing
drew me into a searing moment
melding past and present

Ghostly images forever fixed in my mind

like my gull swooping down
crowning the morning with contradictions

Crumbs

We go on a journey with Hansel and Gretel
follow a trail of crumbs
    left to guide them out of the forest

Trembling siblings fear what lurks in the shadows
    of abandonment
Benumbed by poverty's choking tentacles
parents succumb to the unthinkable

Hypocritical voices broadcast soundbites
  revere life
  protect the fetus
  encourage birthing

Hollow mantra echoes throughout the forest

Hansel and Gretel dismissed
  neglected

Milk, bread... let them follow the crumbs
    CRUMBS
  eaten by grasping Birds

Hansel and Gretel shivering in darkness
    SACRIFICED children in a fairytale

Crouched

Elmer Gantry baptized in bile
            Canonized by sycophants
Strides headlong proselytizing
            a Teflon catechism

Reeking cynicism — infidels' spurn

            Constitutional rights

Targeting the most vulnerable
            Giving a nod to tyranny

Suffering nation pummeled

            Venomous fiats
            Gobbledygook tweets

Flapping in the wind
As happy hour is peddled

            Leaving a populace — crouched

Déjà Vu

Black people in manacles

    Slave labor

woven into the fabric of the economy

Families sundered placed on auction blocks
probed examined — sold like livestock

1865
Constitutional amendment
enslavement skids to an end

1874
    Promise of Reconstruction sours

Vigilantes and supremacists
lying low like bottom fish
feeding on resentment
        SURFACE

Jim Crow: a mincing black stage character
    demeans Black men and women
    with race baiting antics

Segregated toilets...
because white man's shit has no stench

Separate accommodations...
because whiteness adheres
to a superior code of conduct in motels

JUST REWIND

Guard the polls
     DISENFRANCHISE THE OTHER

Create obstacles — bludgeon those who vote
to have their voices heard

Bottom fish feeling the heat
harbor a Jim Crow fantasy bread in the bone

Yin Yang

Walking deadening arid trail
       Hare-brained taboos
Trumpet
       Stereotypical notions

Yin's tears imply femininity
       Yang's harbor effeminacy

       Yin
Lacks physical and mental brawn
       Blurs feminine mystic
       Prone to strident outbursts
       Embraces myth of male superiority

       Yang
Prefers boisterous exhibitionism
       Lacks feminine instincts
       Excoriates gyrating hips
       Touts phallic dominance

       Nature's Whimsy

       Clitoral design
           Mimics penile

Yin and Yang conjoined

Challenge bias
Reject alternate reality

FOSTER SOULFUL CONNECTION

Nakedness

Trust softens vulnerability
    Contour of bodies embracing

    Skipping hearts
    Intertwined legs
    Tangible warmth

Life's encumbrances recede
    Mortality's presence dimmed

      No preening
      No hiding

Nakedness deflates corrosive ego
    Restoring balance

Pretenses dissolve
    Nakedness brings us back to Eden
Unabashedly coupling —

    Poetry enacted in turbulence

    Ending in stillness

Vanishing

Our bodies fuse — dissolve in amniotic fluid

Floating
      No corporal boundaries

Mouths seeking each other's essence
      Like cavefish without sight

Safe in our orgasmic embrace
      Escaping peacock's eyes

Two bodies curled
      Anointing
      Baptizing
      Comingling

Black and White in a colorless mist

Unthinkable

Words hurled
    Like javelins pollute minds

Distorting truth
    Corroding facts
    Leapfrogging

Words weaponized
    Glibly tossed
Into the widening net of social media

    Soundbites
    Lethal slurs
    Gaslighting

Assaulting the threshold of reason

    Provoking
    Beckoning

UNTIL UNTHINKABLE
    BECOMES
      THINKABLE

Searing The Scream into the eyeballs
    of the complicit and indifferent

Crumpled

American flag
  No longer dancing

Blaring bombast
  Fueling scathing assault

Accomplishments

   Scientific Medical Social
    Pooh-poohed

   Research dismissed
    Universities no longer bastions
   Respecting free speech

Expunge history Revise textbooks
  Pluck children from their desks

Target people of color
  Tear the fabric of a diverse vibrant country

Libraries museums cultural venues
  Hijacked

Truth tarnished
Nullified
Trampling American values

Venerating the wizard of oz

As the flag lies crumpled in the sludge

Caesura

When I try to portray *R*…
nesting dolls come to mind for two reasons

He transcended gender keeping
parts of himself hidden
maternal tenderness or masculine ferociousness
tucked away
until a friend's need necessitated
the appearance of one or the other

He reached into his stoical self
when illness rampaged
through his body
impelling him to accept himself
as the giver and receiver of comfort

Time is at a standstill
death's crown approaches

Heads and shoulders drawn together
a moment of stillness
one breathes in
one breathes out

Raised hand surveys a cultivated world
loved and shared

Books of every stamp neatly shelved
CD's reverently
held to avoid smudging precious tracks

His poignant gesture was understood by both

his hand gently touched my forehead
acknowledging the depth of our despair

Solo Flight

I arrived stripped of comforting talisman
No adornments
> photos
> cell phone
>> cast aside
> identity reduced to plasticized ID's

Sensing my presence
> a temple of healing opens

Walking with an attendant
sensitive to the shift shaping lives
> my mind recalls Covid's rampage

In the chokehold of this pestilence
a human stream
>> arrived on gurneys for a solo flight
hovered over by doctors without a flight plan

No protocol manual

ONLY

> medical practice
> compassion
> faith

Hearts swelled in a frantic
struggle with death

Covid's victims would not reach the runway
to the future

My somber thoughts faded
when I was greeted by caregivers
who brought the best of themselves
caring for others

Having faced senseless deaths
      their goal was my safe landing

Sunday Afternoon

Columbus Ave on a Sunday afternoon
Is its own IMAX in real time

It greets the laidback wanderer
With street vendors —
          Sounds   Smells
Waft through the dense summer air

I continue walking North passing a bistro
Teeming with brio —
          Music
Orchestrated by a bandleader
Wearing a signature Panama

Captivated by the music
and joyfulness of the diners

          I pivot

Entering a magnetic field
          I drink deeply from
          an unexpected OASIS

In a split second a sidewalk morphs
into a dance floor

Oliver and Rowena

My retreat is a place to write and enjoy
        early morning air
        usually tranquil and uneventful

But this morning when I lifted my head
to gather words
        my focus shifted
I noticed two robust pigeons —
One jet black — one pale grey
blending into white

Mesmerized by their intimate stance
        playfully touching beaks,
        moving heads side to side

I realized my visitors were seeking a spot
        away from the hubbub

In an instant — black pigeon tenderly
        mounted the receptive female

Separating lead to hanging out and exploring

Like a statue with moving eyes
      I followed them —
Giving them personhood
      Oliver and Rowena
           blithely waddling along
left my haven to rejoin the fray

Untitled

Soothing panther breath on my face
        Midnight blending into ebony

An image of a high-cheek-boned face
                defining strength
                pride like a pharaoh's coin.

Lips puff   whisper   roar

You press your feline body into a welcoming
                she panther
                        infusing warmth

A tender clasp asserts possession.

My Own Chamber

Mulling over
    Newspaper essay

Listening to Alina —
Music not mentioned
    As a prelude to silence

Idleness tiptoes in —
    Modernity's cacophony recedes

Scrambled
    Thoughts
    Emotions
        Surf

Inner voices unfettered
    Chamber
    Operatic
    Symphonic
        Emerge

Confronting

    Life's challenges

Love Death Prejudice Climate revolt
  Global upheaval

In my own chamber clarity reigns

  Cyber chokehold severed

Thoughts liberated
  Words crystalize in poetic form

Rooms Resurrected

Childhood
A place to resurrect rooms inhabited

Bedrooms
Flashbulb memories

A creature looming in the middle of my room
Emitting pungent odor
Especially when being fed kerosene

Stove becomes obsolete
My room expands
Mirrored dresser occupies monster's space

Adornment
Pinky and Blue boy paired on the wall
Behind my bed

Irritating portraits
Depicting an alien world of privilege
Especially when chores come with birthdays

Tidying male sprawl in adjacent bedroom
Tucking sheets

Stumbling upon Playboy magazines
under mattress
Marilyn Monroe more engaging than Pinky

Eyes riveted   Lips mum

Kitchen
Two steps at a time lead to the hub
Spacious kitchen
Radio posing on table
Waiting to be juiced — CLICK
A creaking door opens
Portending ghosts murderers mayhem
Seductive and scary to innocent ears

Mood swings with the speed of light
Astride Silver — The Lone Ranger
vanquishes outlaws
Bringing justice and comfort
Hi-ho-Silver foils Inner Sanctum demons
Banishing nightmares

Kitchen drama
Not on the radio

New gadget
Pressure cooker
Mom in a quandary

Instructions dictate

No Pea Soup
Decides that cannot be

The answer comes when the weight
Flies up in the air and repels

Off the ceiling — as sis and bro take cover
Under the table
Ceiling and wall
Sporting a greenish hue

An explosive pressure cooker
Closes the door on rooms
Alive in the recesses of the mind
Harboring memory

Foisting

Choice subsumed

> Entities creating
>> speed-greed culture
>> strangled in a knot
>> of consumerism

A dizzying merry-go-round peddling
> must-have mentality

Endlessly concocting devices in new versions
> Surreptitiously numbing minds

> Foisting
>> Ghost guns
>> Cell phone addiction
>> AI
>> Cryptocurrency
>> Digital assistants
>> Robocars

All brandished before blurry soulless eyes

Shiny Red Apples

Mindlessly raise the lid of Pandora's box

                              allow

     pungent vapors

                         to escape
                         saturate the air

          giving life to smirky lipped
          demons
    holding hands in a circle

                         celebrating

freedom and morphing into
              benign faces
wearing backpacks

        laden with shiny red apples
              saturated with
                    Prejudice
    Wrath
        Lies
            Greed

Hypocrisy

        Plague   Deceit

      Slick merchants peddling Satan's poisonous
            falsehoods
            to myopic communicants who seal
                 the lid with denial

Lip Smacking

Politicos gnawing-clawing

    Power Brokers

Billionaires and trillionaires

    Wannabe Zillionaires

Heritage tank peddling Fascist Manifesto

Holocaust deniers   climate change deniers

Sensationalism — journalists' new byline

Supreme justices' new motto —
    Quid Pro Quo
Black robes smearing neutrality

Dumb down future voters

Refute science   smother free thought   educate light

Smacking lips break the sound barrier

Blindside and splinter the populace

    SPAWNING   ZOMBIES

High Noon

An onslaught of dizzying bulletins
riddled with invective
        deceit's recipe
quells a populace mesmerized by
                Rat-a-tat tweets
                Slick performances

2025's newly anointed avenger
        lumbers along with blanks
        wearing a hollow crown
        controlling the script
We have spiraled into an alternate reality
        Photo ops with a smudged lens distort —
        undermine clarity

Until the supporting cast develops
        a staunch backbone
                fear and mayhem tighten its grip

Tortured by uncertainty
        Myopic nation spins in a satellite off its axis
—
No ground control
        It is High Noon in America

Breached

Nothing that matters…matters
Words that mattered no longer matter

Doublespeak

Wormlike infiltrates legislative branch

Castrated by worm's inflammatory language
Myopic legislators — anointed with self interest

Leave the constitution riddled with holes
Tipping the balance of power

Weakening the delicate stitching
Binding three branches of government

No patch restoring the framework of democracy
No firewall

Weak-Knead legislators skirt and shuffle
Avoiding worm replicating itself like a virus
In our bloodstream

American Gulag

Cursory deportation
defies norms of law

Cruel   Extreme   Illicit

Tactics

Violate constitutional rights
injecting fear

Hearts   Minds

Sabotaged

Brutal images —

Innocents whisked
to foreign or American

Gulags

Kafkaesque predicament
Stalinesque behavior

Defiling   Looting   Human Rights

Prodding emotions   Roiling consciences

Tattooing swastikas
On American retinas

Alice Speaks

Imagine camera armed
Alice photographing a coterie of women
Clear Comfort becomes stomping ground
>   Rebellious women cavort
>   in cloistered garden

Victorian constraints snubbed
>   Whims indulged
>   Affections uninhibited
>   Male dichotomy ignored

Alice — ventures into realms
defined by maleness
Roving photographer on a bicycle
in a pulsating city
Ever ready camera
Despite hobbling garb

Lured by a world distinct from her own
Alice breaches the cloister
Her camera eye seduced by street life

Compelling people populate
Streets and sidewalks

Newsboys
Postmen
Vendors
Policemen
Beggars —
In a moment of stillness
allow Alice to enshrine them in her lens

Her camera documents their lives —
      Bestowing recognition

Alice speaks to us with her photographs
      Her daring
Discovers different realities

A window into the world at large
with sensibility

Glorify America

History violated
    Horrors of slavery whitewashed

    PURGE

Harriet Tubman — iconic heroine —abolitionist
    Escaped from slavery

Led her people to freedom
    Expunge her achievements

Tuskagee Airman — heroic pilots — WW II
Distinguished service
    15000 sortees never lost a bomber

Suspend Airforce training video referencing
    Tuskagee Airmen — DEI
        Declared Anathema
    As an abhorrent idea — to be squelched

Martin Luther King, Jr.
Civil Rights leader — Non-violent Protests
"I have a dream" still resonates
    Remove his presence from the Oval Office

Toni Morrison — "Beloved" BANNED
    Pulitzer Prize for "Beloved"
    Noble Prize for literature
    An authentic Black Voice
        Captures plight of Black lives in
          America

Sabotage Black History
    Glorify America

Seeking

Humanity challenged
Feels an encroaching horror of an AI world
like a solar storm disrupting connectivity

An AI world has not been spawned from flesh
or earth's loam

Plucking the self from weariness
quelling the turbulent waters of uncertainty
means rejecting rootlessness

Escape virtual chains by suspending self
in nakedness

      Flesh Seeking Flesh

Physical contact instilling calmness tenderness
Accepting corporal communion as transcendent

Knowing that all flesh will feed the earth
equalizes the human condition

      strengthens kinship
      obliterates thoughts of dehumanized
          AI existence

Choose Your Moves

Life — a dance floor
                brimming with possibilities

tango   jitterbug   waltz   salsa
                        free form
                                no pole

male   genderless   female

        partners

                choreographing moves

swinging   swaying
                improvising

                        acclaiming

        diversity   commonality

a kaleidoscopic journey

embracing the dance of life

maneuvering on its challenging surface

endless beginnings   endless choices

denouement

the final dance

Acknowledgements

I'd like to thank Pauline Myrie Stone for being an exuberant cheerleader. Eloine Hall-Oakley for telling me my poems are inspiring. Grace, Ann, and Jan for being steadfast friends and keen listeners. David Nazarro for showing me the way. Thank you to ArtCrawl Harlem's Executive Director, Ulysses Williams, for inviting me to be a poet in residence on Governors Island, and for videoing me reading my poems in relevant art installations. It has been and still is an exhilarating experience to be part of this creative endeavor. Laurie Chandlar for encouraging me to publish More Outbursts and for our smooth and fun-filled interaction. And Kim Killion for the gorgeous cover design, Jennifer Jakes, and the entire team at Killion Group, Inc.

About the Author

Carol Chapman hails from New York City where she taught high school English and a Humanities course in an outreach program for Kingsborough Community College. She spent 20 years at MoMA in the education department before moving to Visitor Services. While at MoMA, Carol contributed to the volunteer newsletter and three of her poems were featured in the summer 2020 issue.

Carol is a lover of poetry, art, music, and exploring New York City's neighborhoods where she interacts with the people and the different rhythms surrounding her. She believes writing poetry is "an act of sharing the drama of the human condition in all its glory and folly." When asked, Carol refers to herself as a scribbler. In 2020, Carol's poem "Kingston Jamaica" —inspired by Fleet Street— was published in *The Jamaica Gleaner*.

Carol's first book *Outbursts: From the Seventh Decade* was published in 2023 and can be found in all major publishing outlets. Carol can be found dancing, traveling, biking on Governors Island, and reading her poems on Instagram @outburstsfromthe7thdecade and GoodReads.

www.ingramcontent.com/pod-product-compliance
Lightning Source LLC
Chambersburg PA
CBHW020549030426
42337CB00013B/1024